Me

What it all means and why Men, young and old, should always embrace being responsible

The Book

J. Gibson

To Dr Cassandra Bradford

Keep on being an amazing woman of purpose!

J. Gibson

MEN = RESPONSIBILITY

Copyright ©2017 by J. Gibson.

Published by 7th Sign Publishing (www.PeauxeticExpressions.com)

All rights reserved. No part of this book may be reproduced or transmitted in any form or by any means without written permission from the author/and or publisher.

ISBN 978-0-692-97358-5

Book Cover Design and Illustrations by David Boyce

Logo Design by J. Gibson

J. Gibson is available for keynote addresses, panel discussions, consultations, church functions, workshop events and radio/TV/internet/podcast interviews. He is also available for any book club meetings, book reviews, parties and events, anywhere in the United States. You can reach him by email at ResponsibilityBook@gmail.com.

Responsibility

[ri-spon-suh-bil-i-tee]

"The state or fact of being responsible, answerable, or accountable for something within one's power, control or management"

Chapter Listing

Acknowledgments and Shout Outs: 7

Introduction: Why This Books Was Written 9

Chapter One: The Meaning Behind The Title 12

Chapter Two: You Made Your Bed, Now Lie In It!
(Life Owes You Nothing) 16

Chapter Three: The Man Was Here First 22

Chapter Four: Not a Race Thing, But a Responsibility Thing..... 26

Chapter Five: Men, Sex and Responsibility 30

Chapter Six: Money and Responsibility 36

Chapter Seven: Women Love a Responsible Man 40

Chapter Eight: A Responsibility to Our Youth of the World...... 48

Chapter Nine: A Responsibility to Forgive 52

Chapter Ten: Take Responsibility And Pride In Your Attire, Fellas
.... 56

Chapter Eleven: A Real Man Wants His Own Stuff 60

Chapter Twelve: She Is NOT a Punching Bag, Fellas…..She is a
Lady 66

Chapter Thirteen: A Responsibility to Be Positive and Stay
Positive 72

Chapter Fourteen: Sacrifice: A Man's Got To Do What A Man's
Got To Do.. 76

Chapter Fifteen: Don't Cheat on Her. Just Be a Man and Tell Her
the Freaking Truth!!! 82

Chapter Sixteen: Why It is Important to Always Be Responsible

.... 88

Chapter Seventeen: No Excuses!!! 92

Bonus Chapter: Never Mind What "They" Think About You, or Say About You... 96

Extra Bonus Chapter: Positive Affirmations to Develop and Maintain a "Responsibility" Mindset

.... 100

Acknowledgements and Shout Outs

First and foremost, I want to thank God for Him blessing me with the gift of writing and giving me this wonderful opportunity and unction to write what I feel is an extremely important, timely, and compelling book. I want to thank my lovely wife, Angela, who is a huge reason this book was able to be come to fruition. Thank you for brainstorming with me over different ideas and chapter topics, and for all of your love and support, my sweet lady. The best is yet to come for you and I.

I want to thank my mother, Evelyn Gibson, for raising me to be the young man that I am, and instilling in me early on in life the importance of manhood and responsibility. Love you ma! I want to give a shout out to all four of my siblings Roberta (Marie Worthie), Debbie, Tony, and Steven. I want to believe that I was a cool big brother growing up, but I know that I was a knucklehead for the most part, and I thank all of you for putting up with me. Love you all.

I want to thank Carlos Harleaux and 7th Sign Publishing. It was an absolute pleasure working with such a professional and prompt person, a true man of integrity and an astute business man. I'm looking forward to working with you for more future literary endeavors.

I want to thank my wonderful mother in law, Linda Carroll, for being an encourager and for sharing my videos on social media. You are quite possibly the best mother in law a man could ask for and forgive me for not telling you this in a while. I want to shout out everyone who was anticipating the release of this written work, my first book. Your patience has been greatly appreciated, and I want you all to enjoy reading this book as much as I enjoyed writing it. On a personal note, if anyone who reads this feels that this book has been a great source of inspiration for you, I want to hear your testimony. Write me at ResponsibilityBook@gmail.com and tell me what you took away from this. Thank you from the bottom of my heart.

Introduction
Why This Book Was Written

Man, when I think about the words written in this book, I get amazed by what I have written, not to toot my own horn, of course. To be completely honest, I really had no intention to write this book in the first place. When I first started this whole *Men=Responsibility* movement, I put those words on a hat and started wearing it everywhere I went. I would get compliments on the hat and people would ask me what *Men=Responsibility* meant. I would explain that I just feel I have a personal mandate to promote manhood and responsibility in our society.

This is what is missing in America, as I truly believe this, with all my heart. Mostly it would be women who would complement me. Some would tell me that it should be men and women accepting responsibility. While I agree with that, my primary focus is on pushing for more men to be responsible, because I am a man and I want to see more men do better, for a better society. I want to see men be better fathers to their kids, better husbands to their wives, better providers for their families, better police officers for protecting the public, and more importantly, I want to see men accepting more responsibility in their lives.

Any real man has to understand that being a man comes with responsibility for so much, because as men, we are the catalysts in this world. We are looked to as the foundation of creations. That is just the basic plain truth. Now, how I came to actually write this book is amazing. One day while preparing to put my car in the shop for some repairs, I stopped at a popular burger spot in the heart of Dallas, Texas. I was sitting at a booth, getting ready to receive my food and this guy comes in the restaurant and orders a couple of milkshakes to go. He looks over and sees me sitting in the booth, wearing my hat and he comes over to ask me about *Men=Responsibility*.

He tells me that he noticed the car magnets on my vehicle that say *Men=Responsibility* when he drove up, therefore, he wanted to know what it meant. I go into my spill about my viewpoint and beliefs, and he's impressed with my explanation, as far as I can tell. We start talking about the change in our society; how it seems that men have regressed from being responsible, in so many areas.

I tell him about my hats and while he liked the hats, he did not want to purchase one. But here's the thing, he reached into his wallet and pulled out money to purchase the hat without wanting a hat, which really moved me. I wanted that guy to walk away with something for his money, but all I had at the time were the hats. That is when I dug deep into my mind and thought about what else I could have to offer to people in promoting this movement. That is when it hit me to write a book, to better explain what *Men=Responsibility* means.

I absolutely love writing and I figured why not write a book that I believe many would want to read. So here in this book is where I believe will give the best explanation from my mindset of what *Men=Responsibility* means. It's my hope that you will take a lot from it in a positive way: one that will definitely help those who want to grow into better, more responsible men, both young and old.

Be well and enjoy…..

J. Gibson

Chapter One
"The Meaning Behind The Title"

This is how *Men=Responsibility* all started:

In some circles of people that know me and know how I like to express myself, I'm known as the "Awareness Guy". When I would attend different vendor functions where I would show off and sell my "End the Madness" message necklaces, I was all about bringing awareness to the masses highlighting such issues that affect this society. I have such a 'knack for promoting something with a message behind it', is what people would say to me. Thus, one day, I embarked upon creating hats with a variety of select positive and uplifting messages and sayings printed on the hats. Out of the blue, it just came to me, "Men=Responsibility".

Now, why would I put those words on a hat? Well, I'm all about promoting manhood. I love it when men are doing things that show that they are real men; making every effort to be positive in their lives. On the flip side, I have increasingly begun to notice that many men, young and old, are not being positive. They are not promoting responsibility. When I see something that I feel should be promoted, I'll step up and start the ball rolling, to get that particular thing promoted immediately. Responsibility is something we all should care about, and it is something we all should want to see instilled in our men, and women for that matter. But honestly, I'm more passionate about seeing men be more responsible.

Simply because I am a man, and as a man I aspire to see other men doing more of what they're supposed to be doing, on a regular basis. I also realize that as men, we're the catalysts of everything that happens on this planet. We're the decision makers, the builders and construction workers, the heavy-lifters and world leaders. This is who we are as men.

With these things comes that massive word, "responsibility". We as men are bombarded with responsibility on a daily basis. As you read this book, you will see why this is the case for men. Think about the president of the United States. That office is the most important office in America. There is not one day that goes by without us seeing something in the news that involves the president, whether it is negotiating with foreign leaders or conducting seemingly endless trade talks, and so forth: the president's job is to ultimately perform those duties that result in the overall good for the country he serves.

The person who holds this office has a ton of responsibility on his shoulders, constantly. He knows the magnitude of responsibility that comes every day with being the leader of the free world and we should hope that he embraces it with vigor and strength. I'm sure one day when we have our first woman president; she will see the huge responsibility of that position as well. When people see *Men=Responsibility* on a hat that I'm wearing, or on my magnetic car sign, they appear to be both puzzled and surprised... most of the time I find this to be quite amusing. I have even had one guy stop me in the street and have me pull over so that I could explain the sign.

After I explained what my interpretation of this meant, he happily purchased a hat and I made a new friend in the process.

Now, let me explain to you, the reader, what this means from my own vantage point. It means that if a man is going to be a real man in this world, then he has to understand that as a man, he has to be RESPONSIBLE. "Responsible for what?" you may ask... and that's just it...responsible in every aspect of being a man. As men we are decision makers, trailblazers, providers and builders. There are so many aspects of responsibility entangled in all of these things. Understand this, when you see *Men=Responsibility*, you should see something that many can relate to and understand.

For the most part, one of the main reasons I'm encouraging this is because irresponsibility has completely overrun and overtaken our society, by leaps and bounds. When you really think about it, it's getting worse as the days go by. You see irresponsibility on television, on the internet (i.e. "WorldStar, Media Takeout), and in so many other places and spaces in the land. I can't speak for anyone else, but as for me, I'm tired of seeing this in so many of our men, both young and old. I have decided to speak out against it. In turn, I have written this book in an attempt to show why it's vitally important to restore a sense of responsibility in the hearts of men everywhere.

Some have said to me that everyone needs to be more responsible. While I wholeheartedly agree with that sentiment, I'm focusing primarily on men, because again, we men are the catalyst of life and progression: it's our job as men to be responsible, because when we're responsible, our women and children will see us as the leaders we're supposed to be. As a result, things tend to turn out right and the ebb and flow progresses smoothly.

As you continue to read the chapters and turn the pages of this book, it is my hope and desire that change can and will be made for the overall improvement of our society. It is my hope that a desire to be more responsible will explode within all who read this book. I may have repeated some things in this chapter, but hopefully you can see the seriousness in why I'm promoting responsibility in men. Some things have to be reiterated more than once, to drive the point home.

Chapter Two
You Made Your Bed... Now Lie in It!
(Life Owes You Nothing)

This is what I would call a great opening line to what being personally responsible in your life means. In 2009, I attended Le Cordon Bleu culinary school in Dallas, Texas. I must say that that was a wonderful experience in my life. I made some good friends, and the process that I went through to learn how to cook and why certain dishes were made like they are was fun and exciting. The length of time it took for me to complete my schooling was about a year and a half, and I had to get student loans to attend school.

I graduated with honors. Post graduation, I went on to have some great experiences, completing catering jobs and working in different restaurants, acquiring even more additional new cooking techniques. Fast forward to many years later and here I am just now starting to pay on my student loans. Yes, I know, I should not have allowed myself to get that deep in the student loan hole, but I'm taking care of my business now and that's what counts.

Why did I bother mention all of this? I wanted to show that it's never too late to embrace being responsible. Amazingly, I'm really not into cooking! At the present time, being a world class chef, somewhat due to the surgery I had for scoliosis on my spinal column, over 20 years ago, resulting in a challenge for me to stand on my feet for long periods of time in a kitchen. This is an unwelcomed hindrance in my life. But, in spite of that, I made my bed by obtaining a student loan for culinary school, and now I have to lie in it and pay what I owe.

You see, even though I really don't want to pay back this loan (just being honest), I would be a hypocrite in telling others to be responsible in their lives and I know that I have an obligation myself and to not honor that obligation would not be right. As a man, you have an obligation, you have a responsibility to honor those obligations, no matter how big or small they may be. As a matter of a fact, when you choose to be irresponsible and not honor your obligations, that lack of responsibility can affect your future.

Hear me and hear me good fellas, when you make your beds in life, you have the responsibility to lie in those beds and to take care of whatever obligations you create. No one else can do that for you, and if you're a real man, you should not want anyone else to take care of what you should take care of. Bottom line, a real man is going to take care of his responsibilities, no matter how hard they may be. Also, a real man has to understand that no matter how hard things may be at any given moment in his life, he can NOT ever stop being responsible, because being responsible is the essence of being a man.

I was watching an online talk show one day, and the segment that was on was about helping a couple get back the trust in their marriage, due to a betrayal. The situation was that of a man who had a family and at one point in his life, things got tough for him; he lost his job. His wife was a stay-at-home mom: his income was the only income that they had to live on. They had a minimal amount of savings in the bank, but not enough to live on for the duration of time it took while he looked for work. So, the decision was made that they would move back in with his mother for a little while until he could find work, since they could not afford to pay the rent any longer where they were living.

At some point, while they were living at his mother's home, the wife complained to the talk show host that she felt her husband had reverted back to acting like a teenager; going places with his mother, leaving her at the house, and not really diligently looking for work so that they could eventually move out and get their own place again. She felt that he stopped being responsible to her and their family. Thus, she eventually met another man on the internet and confided in him about what was happening in her life.

As you can imagine, she did more that confide in this man, whoever he was. She ended up cheating on her husband, and I believe she carried on a short affair with the other man until the husband found out. He, of course, was pissed and devastated, resulting in their separation from each other for a short while, until they decided to seek counseling to save their fractured marriage.

The show host asked his wife why did she seek comfort from another man, and she confessed that she felt her husband stopped being a husband to her once they moved back in with his mother. She felt that he temporarily abandoned his responsibilities as a husband to her and a father to their kids; that he took losing his job really hard, and once they moved in with his mother, he lost his focus and got comfortable being back at home. The husband felt that the wife should have been more understanding about what was happening, and the wife said that she was sympathetic. But, then she said to her husband that as the leader of their family, he should have maintained his focus on being the leader and not acting like he was 15 again.

I believe that the husband decided that he wanted to work things out with his wife and save their marriage. The overall reason as to why I added this story here is to show you, the reader, that as a man, no matter how difficult things may get, no matter what challenges show up in your life, that you as a man can NEVER stop being responsible, especially if you have a family that depends on you to be a strong-willed and dependable man. That is how it is fellas. Please know that no matter what, when we make our beds, we have to lie in them, not run away like little boys. Because not only is that not fair to you as a man, that's not fair to the people who depend on you to never stop being responsible.

In addition, you have to understand that you will be knocked down and kicked in your butt sometimes in life. When that happens, you have to get up and keep going and keep living, because life owes you nothing. You can't have a "woe is me" attitude whenever things get hard... and they do tend to get hard at times. At the end of the day, having an attitude of despair and self-pity will get you nothing. Only hard work, action, believing in yourself and moving in a direction of faith will get you want you need and desire in this life, and nothing else.

Whatever you do, don't expect people to feel sorry for you, not even your family. A man, at some point, has to learn to stand on his own two feet. He has to learn to be responsible for his own life, because no one else is going to be responsible for a grown person's life. Please take what I said in this chapter to heart, fellas. And ladies, you too can take from this. Life owes you nothing, so whatever beds you make in your life, always be prepared to lie in them and take responsibility for your own lives. You can do it!!

Chapter Three
The Man Was Here First

Without trying to get all religious on you, when God created the Heavens and the Earth, he created the man first. He gave the man, Adam, a responsibility to tend to the garden and everything that was in it. And when God noticed that Adam needed a companion, He took out of Adam a rib and created the woman, Eve. Fast forward a little bit, and the serpent came to Eve and told her that she could eat of the tree that God forbade her and Adam to touch, or they would die.

Well, as the story goes, Eve did indeed touch the tree, ate the fruit, and gave a piece of fruit to Adam and he ate it as well. Why am I going here, you may ask? Well, it's simple. Adam was the man of that union, the first human being in existence on the scene, and he had a staunch responsibility to see to it that neither he nor Eve disobeyed God and touch what God forbade them to touch. When God came calling in the garden, who was He calling for? He was calling for Adam, because Adam was the one that God put in charge of everything, including the woman that God gave him. And when Adam responded the way he did by hiding, God held him accountable, not the woman. Adam was held responsible for not doing what God had instructed.

The one that God had created first and foremost was the <u>man</u>. But because of Adam's lack of responsibility and accountability for this serious situation and for making sure that neither he nor Eve touched that one tree that they were forbidden to touch, the fall of man occurred. You see, God put man here on the earth first, and then he gave man the gift of woman. And yes, I say proudly that God's greatest gift to man is the woman. When God did that, he did that with the thought in mind that man would be responsible for that woman, and as history has shown us, man has failed miserably in that sense.

When you look at the current state of our society, that cycle of failure in our men is happening right now, seemingly on a perpetual basis. What I've come to understand is that when it comes to being responsible, especially for our families, it ultimately falls on the shoulders of the man. It will always fall on the shoulders of the man, because that is the correct order of things.

There was a TV court show that I use to love watching by the name of "Judge Joe Brown", and he had a saying that he would always recite during most of his arbitrary cases. He would always say "Protecting womanhood, and promoting manhood". I would just love it when he said that: it made so much sense. I'll try to explain what I believe he meant by saying that. I believe he was saying that we men have an obligation to be responsible for our families and our society, as we are appointed to be, the stronger, dominant sex; to protect and care for our women, the weaker sex. What I would especially notice watching some of the Judge Joe Brown episodes, is you'd see a man acting somewhat less than a man...being sued by an ex-girlfriend, his mama, or some other relative or former friend, with the end result culminating in the fact that the case boiled down to him not taking responsibility for his actions, whatever those actions were.

Imagine this: if most men out here would simply step up their 'manhood' game and become more responsible, a lot of these small claims court shows we watch would probably be diminished or cancelled, because men would be taking care of business and being responsible. Wouldn't that be nice? On a personal note, I miss seeing Joe Brown on TV, spitting that sage wisdom on these young and impressionable men. That is what's missing out here, big time. All in all, the mere fact that men were put on this earth first lets us know that men have a sole responsibility to be accountable, in every sense of living. When men are responsible, everything else falls in place. Think about this as you continue to turn the pages of this book.

Chapter Four
Not a Race Thing, But a Responsibility Thing

Now, when it comes to being responsible, this most certainly is not about any certain race. It doesn't matter if you're white, black, yellow, purple or whatever, all men should want to be responsible. What you have to understand is that no matter what part of the world you live in, as a man, responsibility is paramount in your life, and if it's not, it definitely should be. There are irresponsible men in all shades, hues, complexions, you name it.

Unfortunately, what we see in the media and on the internet is a push to promote a narrative that shows certain races that are more irresponsible than that of others, and vice versa. To be more frank, we see black men/men of color that are shown in a bad light more often than other men. As a black man, I see this constantly and it's truly tiresome.

A great example of this disparity is portrayed quite often whenever I watch Maury Povich on television, which is not often, let me tell you. Now this show has been on the air for what seems like an eternity. What has kept this show on for so long are those words that people love hearing Maury says? "You are the father/you are NOT the father!!" Funny to some, sad to others, I know. However, do you know what is even crazier? This type of programing tends to show more black people than they do any other race, and I believe that this is the reason.

The producers of these shows know that some black people have a tendency to be more animated than other races of people. And, of course, we know that animated people equal television ratings... and what's a trashy TV show without those coveted ratings? Maury is not the only culprit in this regard. You can turn on any channel on your television at any given moment that show these reality shows, and you will undoubtedly see black people, more than any other race of people, cursing each other, fighting, throwing chairs and drinks and punches, and not exactly in that order.

Let me break it down to you. Even though this seems to be a reality, it's not. Open your eyes and you're bound to see a ton of men, no matter what color they are, being irresponsible. What is even more tragic about this is that there are men who <u>choose,</u> yes choose, to ditch being responsible, no matter how big of a mess they have created. I've seen white guys totally walk away from a woman they've impregnated, with them saying that she should have been more careful and she should have used birth control. We all see it in so many more examples that can fill up the pages in this book.

Another example that I will use where it seems that irresponsibility has been rewarded is MTV's "Teen Mom". For some crazy reason, that has been on that network for a long time. Now I will admit that I've never sat and watched an episode of this show, for that I have better things to do with my time than to watch young adolescent white people prepare for an unplanned pregnancy. But I bring this up as an example to show that irresponsibility is all around, no matter what race the people are who are not being responsible.

The people on this particular show are paid for not being responsible. Makes you realize how low we've become as a society. This is what I want to say, that no matter how hard television, the media, Hollywood producers, or any other entity will try to convince you, there is no such thing as one race of people not being more responsible than another race. You will see irresponsible behavior equally being carried out in all races.

Yes, I'm a black man, and I see a ton of black men being irresponsible on a regular basis, but then I also see white men, Asian men, Mexican men, African men, and so on, being irresponsible on a regular basis. When I promote *Men=Responsibility*, guess what? I am referring to ALL men, no matter what his race is. It should be everyone's desire to see men do better and be more responsible, that is all men in the "human" race. And while I'm at it, responsibility is not confined to being a liberal, conservative, independent, libertarian, democrat, republican, or any specific political affiliation. It's all encompassing, to all men, period.

Chapter Five
Sex, Men and Responsibility

Now this chapter will be a hard hitting one, and it has to be, because men love sex, me included. Once a man reaches a certain age, he begins to notice women, their bodies and shapes, and his mind runs wild with thoughts of endless sexual gratification. That's fine and dandy, as biology meant it to be that way, but what so many men have failed to realize is when you have sex with a woman, you absolutely have to be responsible about it. What do I mean you ask? I mean that men for the most part tend to only think with the head in their pants, and not the one on their shoulders when it comes to "getting some".

This type of thinking has caused many men to fall. Yes, I said fall and in most cases, fall hard. I'm going to say something that some would view as controversial, but I said that this chapter would be hard-hitting, so here goes: a man should not ever have unprotected sex with a woman that he's not married to. Let me repeat myself; a man should not ever have unprotected sex with a woman that he's not married to. When a man engages in that type of behavior, he's not being responsible and here's why. Unprotected sex always leads to unplanned pregnancies, especially if the woman is fertile as all get out, or an STD can be passed from one person to the next, and in some cases, both of these can occur.

Let's talk about the unplanned pregnancies. For some reason, when unmarried people have sex, and a pregnancy happens, the man sometimes doesn't feel an obligation to stick around and prepare to be in the child's life. Think about that show I mentioned in the last chapter, "Maury". One of the show's most popular premises are women who come on, looking to see which man that she has slept with and engaged in unprotected sex with, and ultimately not being sure of who the father of her child may be. Then some man will come on, screaming and yelling from backstage that he's not the father, but never denying that he slept with her or denying that the sex they engaged in was unprotected.

All of this craziness going on between these people, all the while you have children being born in this madness, when most of this could have been avoided had the people engaging in the sexual acts just been responsible. Now, even though it takes two to tango, I personally feel that the "men" should take the initiative and employ birth control. Why? Because let's face it, men hardly ever turn down the chance for sex. Most men are in sexual overdrive all of the time, and when the opportunity presents itself for a man to have sex, you can believe he's going to take it. But in doing so, that man should be responsible and put on a condom, whether that woman is on the pill or not.

I've heard men say, "I don't like wearing condoms, I can't feel anything". I would say to those men, "do you like having your paycheck shrunk due to child support, my man?" Think about all of the professional athletes we see with multiple children by multiple women. They have money, lots of it, and that money attracts women, lots of women. Despite having above average income, those men still have an obligation to be responsible to not allow themselves to be caught up by a fine body and a pretty face. Let's be real about this. Most of the women these guys meet don't really care about the athlete, all they care about is the money and how they can get their hands on that money, even if it means getting pregnant on purpose to make it happen. There are so many stories about pro ball players having kids, and the women doing what they can to make that athlete's life a living hell, all for money.

You would think that with all of the money they make playing a sport, they would be more careful and keep a stash of condoms with them always, but you'd be wrong. Like I said earlier, when it comes to sex, most men think with the little head below their waist instead of the big one on their shoulders, and that must change at some point.

On a personal note, I was not a virgin when I got married. I enjoyed sex, and not to brag in the least bit, but I was responsible about my sexual pleasures, and I wore a condom for the most part. And because I was responsible, I never contracted an STD, and thankfully there was never a situation where I was about to be a father when I wasn't ready to be one. You see, because I was responsible when I was younger, I now enjoy life free from the stresses that being irresponsible could have brought me.

It is my sincere desire that men would learn to be responsible when it comes to having sex. Truthfully, good sex may only last about 30 minutes, but the pain and anguish that it can bring can last for years and years. For example, I have a female friend who met this lady at a women's get together years ago, and my friend told me about what this particular lady shared with everyone who was in attendance. Now, you know that when women get together, they tend to talk about two things: men and their kids. This lady in particular talked about her life and how she was married to a man who had four babies' mothers.

That's right... her husband had four kids by four different women. Amazingly, this lady said that she was on good terms with all four of the women. Well, the downside she talked about, of course, was the fact that her husband has to pay child support for the children he shares with those ladies; not to mention that they have two kids of their own to raise and support financially.

According to my friend, the lady was really upset with her husband because she felt he was not ambitious enough to get a better paying job, so that the financial burden would not be so great, due to the fact that his checks were low, thanks to all of the child support the state would deduct from his paychecks every pay period. She described that their money was always insufficient for their own household needs and desires.

I mentioned this ~~up~~ to demonstrate that this is a glaring example of not being responsible with it comes to a man and his sexual exploits. This guy had a baby with pretty much every woman he was with before he got married and now his track record of not being responsible has been affecting his present situation. I don't have a clue as to who this man could be, but I would have to imagine that although he more than likely loves his kids, if he could go back and do it again, I'm sure he would have been more

33

careful and more responsible and employed birth control every time he had sex.

This is my desire, for all unmarried men out here, to be more careful and more responsible. I know that this is wishful thinking, but it's possible. Now, let's take a look at the very real possibility of acquiring STD's. When a man has unprotected sex with someone who's not his spouse, he's playing with fire. There are sexually transmitted diseases out there that anyone can be carrying; Gonorrhea, chlamydia, herpes, syphilis, and the deadly HIV/AIDS. You would have to be a fool to want any of these STD's.

He doesn't know who she has been with, and vice versa. You can't tell if a person is carrying a disease based on how they look. A man can get with the prettiest woman on the block, and there are plenty of pretty women out here, and if she's offering up herself on a silver platter, he will probably feel like he's hit the lottery. But fellas, be careful!! No matter what she tells you, no matter how fine and physically attractive she may be, you have the obligation to be responsible and wrap it up. It is not worth it to have unprotected sex, because if you do, you will most likely pay a price.

Condoms can be a man's best friend, but only if he allows them to be. ~~and~~ I'll add this as well: many of these men should embrace abstinence, because condoms don't always protect you from STD's. Some sexually transmitted diseases can infect you despite wearing a prophylactic during sexual activity. I had to put that out there. Bottom line, you owe it to yourselves, men, to be more responsible with your penis. If you're not careful, you're bound to contract something that you don't want, sooner or later. STD's don't care who you are, what your social status in life is, or how much money you have in the bank. So much is riding on that (no pun intended), including your life and your finances.

Chapter Six
Money and Responsibility

I'm sure you've all heard the saying "a fool and his money are soon parted". I would say that many of us can agree with this, because when it comes to money, many men are not responsible. In addition to being a novice culinary practitioner, I have a background in sales, car sales to be exact. When I first started selling cars, I would meet many seasoned salesmen who were making great money on a monthly basis. I'm talking five figures every four weeks.

Occasionally, I would have conversations with these guys about the money they were making selling cars and some of the things they would do with their money. Boy, what I heard was crazy. I'm talking regular strip club visits, jewelry, car rims, constant restaurant visits, and women galore. Now, I'm not saying that these men were wrong to do those things, because we're talking about grown men who spent and circulated dollars how they saw fit, which is every man's right. But what happens when some men started going overboard and their spending habits became a bit reckless and irresponsible? That is the point of this chapter; to attempt to explain how being financially irresponsible can wreck one's life.

One manager I worked for recently explained to me that when he first started selling cars, he was pulling in over $10,000 a month, and he was in his early 20's. He explained to me that he was living high on the hog around that time; spending money on things he thought would make his life better. But then he told me that as he got older and he had a chance to reflect, he was full of regret, regarding how he was spending his salary at the time. He told me that he should have been more responsible and not spent so frivolously on "bull crap". These were his exact words to me that day. He ended up telling me that if he could go back in time and get back all the money he spent in his younger years, he would have over $100,000 in the bank.

He was making great money, but as soon as he got it, he felt the need to spend it, as soon as the check cleared. Think about this one question fellas; can many of you relate to this guy, spending money on things you don't need or can do without? Ask yourself this question. Just how responsible am I with money? Can your family depend on you to be responsible with money to pay the bills on time? One reason why it is so important to be responsible with money is because it's gone beyond the point that the money we have is just as important as the precious air we breathe.

We can't do without either of these things, money and air, it's that simple. If you can't trust yourself to be responsible with your money, you can't very well expect a wife, girlfriend, kids, a business partner or bill collectors to depend on you. And those bill collectors: they want their money on time, every time, rain or shine. I encourage each and every man reading this chapter to wise up and take inventory of the things they spend their money on. If it's something you can use over and over again after it's purchased, it's an asset for sure. But if it's something that you will probably get bored with within a month after it's purchased, it's probably a liability, and you don't need it. Of course, you should want to enjoy life, but make certain that your tomorrows are not affected negatively by the goods or services you buy today. Be smart with your dollars, men.

One last point I want to make. One of the quickest ways that rich people tend to go broke is by living a life of excess where they're purchasing things just so that they can impress other people. What I mean is that they'll drive a certain car, or live in a certain pricey neighborhood or wear all name brand clothing, all just to look a certain way for people. Let me tell you, that is a pointless and flat out dumb way to live your life. First of all, those people that you're trying to impress, they could really care less about what you have. Bottom line, they don't care about your houses, cars, fine clothes, or any other opulent items you have in your possession.

Also, I guarantee you that if you were to somehow fall on hard times and lose your fortune, all while trying to "keep up with the Joneses", those people you were trying so hard to impress won't lift a finger to help you out in your time of despair. They'll probably laugh at you and talk about you like a dog behind your back, all because you were not responsible about how you dispersed and circulated your dollars, and because you cared about what others thought about you. My humble advice to you, my friend, is to say be more responsible with your money: ~~and~~ forget trying to impress people. Live life on your own terms, ~~and~~ not on anyone else's.

Chapter Seven
Women Love a Responsible Man

Check this out. I posted these words on my Facebook page some months ago, before I ever thought about writing this book, and the response was overwhelmingly wonderful. So I'm going to say this and hopefully many of you phenomenal men will get it.

<u>The best aphrodisiac a man can give a woman is not Spanish fly, or any other sexual stimulant you can buy from the erotica store. Not even the expensive brand name cologne you wear is the best aphrodisiac for many women. No, the best aphrodisiac a man can ever give a woman is for him to show her that he is responsible, in every sense of the word. A responsible man will turn a woman on every time, without fail</u>

You have read this right. Responsibility as an aphrodisiac will never steer you wrong when it comes to getting and keeping the ladies. As I wrote in chapter three, men were here in existence first, and because that is the case, it is up to men to put a woman's mind at ease by being responsible and accountable. What I mean by that is this; the man is responsible to maintain employment, responsible to pay the mortgage/rent, on time and every time, pay the bills, be good providers, pay for dates, and so forth... to do all the things that men do, or are supposed to do.

By being accountable I am referring to being able to show the woman that he is not a "playboy": that he is accountable to her and her only. A woman's role in a relationship is to be a "helper"; that is when things tend to get tough for the man, the woman decides to help him out. But, that woman should not be put in a bind, where she's in the relationship, carrying most of the load for that relationship. I can state as a fact, that if a woman sees a man and observes how he is before they exchange vows, that will be a huge determining factor to that woman as to whether or not she feels that this man is worth marrying.

Think of it like this: A woman can meet a seemingly great man, one who has the body of a Greek God, drives a nice car and has money longer than the Nile River (these are the types of things that would normally attract most women to a man), but, just let that lady of caliber take the time to get to know the actual irresponsibility and immaturity of that particular man, by spending time with him... she will soon start to see him in a different light.

Once she starts to notice that he's not all that responsible in paying bills on time, or he demonstrates irresponsibility in other areas of his life, she will then begin to back away from him, nice body and all. Why? Well the key word here again is "responsibility". In spite of his nice body, handsome face, nice bank account and whatever else he has, at some point, she will want to see him as a responsible man. His being accountable, dependable and trustworthy is what will keep that woman with that man. All of his material possessions won't be enough, no matter how opulent they may be, if he is not a responsible man, in her eyes he is not a real man. He will undoubtedly begin to display traits of unreliability, those that will annoy her to no end. Trust me, no decent woman will be with him for long. Speaking from experience, there was a time when I was not all in as a responsible man. One of my exes from a long time ago was paying for our dates.

She was doing the things that I should have been doing in our relationship. It ultimately took a toll on our union; it stung me as a man. Needless to say, we eventually stopped seeing each other. Looking back on it now, I can see that I should have stepped up my game. I should have been a bit more ambitious in my life, and gotten a job that paid me more than what I was making at the time. and My ex would not have had to carry us for as long as she did. She was a real sweetheart for doing that, but it went on longer than it should have, with that being completely on me.

Don't get me wrong, I'm not saying that a woman shouldn't support the man she's with, but there should be some boundaries in that support. He should recognize his role as the dominant, take-charge figure, with the female; the pillar of his existence, being able to pick up the slack, whenever the need warrants. What is seen in today's landscape is the perpetual picture of the men being the followers as the women lead. In the original, God-created design of a relationship/marriage, the man lead and the woman followed. In other words, if that man desires to be with a woman, then he has a responsibility to show her that he's worthy of her companionship: he has a responsibility to show her that he can be the leader she will come to admire.

Let's be honest: no real woman wants to take care of a grown man. This is not the divine order of things in life. Irresponsibility in a man is a major turnoff to a woman. Most women, if not all women, want to feel that they are with a man who has leadership qualities. She doesn't want to feel like she's leading him, and any self-respecting woman who finds herself in such a relationship will be looking for the exit. Again, if a woman has to constantly tell a man to be responsible and to be a man, pretty soon she's not going to want to be with that man.

Her desire is to be with a man who is responsible, who doesn't need to be told what to do every 10 minutes, of every day. She will desire and admire the man who takes the initiative to make sure that things are taken care of. Her desire is to be with a grown, able-bodied, responsible man: not a little boy who still needs his mommy. She definitely doesn't want to be with a man that is still living at his parent's home. *(As a side note: fellas, if you are living in a home with your parents, make sure that it's your home, not theirs).*

Here's another point I want men to consider. A responsible man will almost never have to worry about a nagging woman. I have found that in most relationships, when a man is being nagged by his wife/girlfriend, it's mainly because he's not doing something that he should be doing. Women want to be put at ease by the man she's with. In other words, women love comfort and security. If she's with a man who is not providing either of these things, she's going to give him grief over that. Men, you can forget about getting SEX from your woman, if she is constantly nagging you about something.

A woman's emotions are involved, for the most part, when sex happens. If she is pissed off or angry with you for your lack of responsibility, or something else along those lines, she will not be emotionally vested in giving you what you desire. But, when you are responsible and you're doing things to put her mind in a place of comfort, then not only will she not nag you, she'll be putty in your hands, giving you all that you want and desire from her, especially SEX.

When I say that women love a responsible man, this is not a joke. This is real talk. The woman is your gift, fellas. You have to constantly give her reminders as to why she is wanted by you and with you. This is how it used to be once upon a time, but somewhere along the line that stopped being the case for men and women. We need to get back to this, for harmonious relationships/marriages to thrive and succeed. This is why it's so important for young men to have fathers and strong male role models in their lives; to show them how to engage women, so that when they get to an age of accountability, they'll know that being responsible is the right way to go. All in all, a woman is most comfortable when she's with a man who is a 100% responsible man. Anything less than that is not acceptable to a woman.

We've got to get back to doing those small, yet powerful things that turn women on. What do I mean, you ask? I am referring to things like pulling her chair out from the table when you both arrive at a restaurant. Also, opening the car door for her, as she enters and exits, when you both go for a drive, anywhere around the city and beyond, is something she will appreciate.

Now this is a big one: fellas, you have to be verbal with the ladies. They just love it when you express out loud how good they look, or how wonderful that meal they prepared for you was, consistently including how much you love them. Women need and desire daily confirmations of affection from their men. It's a little difficult to explain further, just know that's the way it is. We have to be responsible in the big things, as well as the little things, when it comes to our women. As I have previously stated, women love a responsible man. This is the truth, guys. Therefore, run with this and impress the ladies!

As one final point in this chapter, you are NOT a real man if you are allowing a woman to finance your way of living. You cannot call yourself a man if you are not financing your own lifestyle. There are many relationships happening right now where the man is allowing his woman (or women) pay for everything he has, whether it is the car he drives, ~~or~~ the clothes he wears, or by paying his rent or mortgage, if a man is able-bodied and in his right mind, he should be paying for these things with his own money. He has to be fully responsible in this regard. If he's not, he is a sorry excuse of a man, bottom line. Women love a responsible man. So, if you are not living a life of responsibility, you had better make a 180 degree change, my man. If you're going to call yourself a man, then act and live like a real man, a responsible man.

Chapter Eight
A Responsibility to Our Youth of the World

This is the pinnacle of why it's important to be responsible and to maintain responsibility in our world. When we as men are responsible, that trait of being responsible tends to fall on the young people, our future. Young people are sponges and they soak up and emulate the things they see the older folks do. For example, there are a bunch of young men out here not being responsible fathers to the children that they helped create, not paying child support or spending time with their kids. In most cases, this is a learned behavior, one that they've acquired from their fathers.

Yes, their fathers were not in their lives, their fathers did not spend time with them, take them to the park and played catch. Their fathers did none of those things. As a result, they had no great example of what it means to be a father. So they continue the sad cycle they were exposed to. It is my hope and desire that we can begin to end this cycle, but, it has to be a concentrated effort on all of our parts, as men. Speaking for myself, I would say that I had a pretty decent upbringing, although I wish things could have been much better than they were.

I was reared in a single parent home, with my mother being the only parent to raise five kids, all on her own. My father, as much as I loved him, was not a responsible man, with regard to helping raise us and being a strong presence in our lives. My sincere wish would have been for my father to be an integral part in our lives, but unfortunately, that was not to be the case. I will give my mother credit for teaching her kids to be responsible, both her sons and daughters. But what would it have been like if my father would have been there to teach us some things our mother could not? What would it have been like for our father, the man who helped create us, to teach his sons how to be men, and to teach his daughters what to expect from a man? Sadly, we will never know.

I can only surmise that this is how it was supposed to have been. It was tough for me, in particular, not to have my father teach me how to shave, how to tie a tie, or how to change the oil in a car. I made it to manhood without a father there to guide me and I believe I turned out okay. But, I truly believe that having a father there would have made a huge difference. I have had many guy friends who pretty much went through the same thing I did: they did not have their fathers in their lives. This is something that has to stop. Some of those same guys are doing the exact same things that their fathers did. They will have kids with a woman, only to turn around and pretend that those babies don't exist.

I don't have children at the moment, but if I did, I could not do to them what was done to me. I know that my kids would be my world and my full responsibility. ~~and~~ I would happily embrace that responsibility, through the good times and through the tough, trying times. One thing I try to do is teach young people the importance of being responsible for their actions at an early age. This is something that we all have a responsibility to do. To all of the fellas that have children, if you're one of the men in this society that are not active participants in the lives of

49

your children, I strongly encourage you to change your ways.

Please, redirect the negative trend. I beg you to play active roles in their lives, because they do need you. They may not come out and say it, but, they may be screaming for your attention, sometimes in destructive ways. Either way, you have a responsibility to be a father to your kids. You have a responsibility to nurture their minds, to protect them from evil forces that are in the world, to raise them to eventually become productive and responsible citizens; those that society can use for positive things. To the fellas that have no children, but you have a heart to help the youth, I encourage you to consider mentorship programs.

There are literally thousands of young men and women who are fatherless, and could use a great, wonderful and responsible role model in their lives, so that they can know how to conduct themselves, both in public and private, ~~out here~~ as responsible people. Young people who don't know any better, need their minds cultivated and shaped properly; it is up to us older, mature men to do so. If we don't help carry this out, who will? We have a responsibility to teach our young people the importance of being responsible, and in turn, they'll teach the next generation, thus that positive cycle will continue. But it has to start now. We've have got a lot of work to do, men!!!

Chapter Nine
A Responsibility to Forgive

Let's face it everyone, life can be mean, cruel, vicious and sometimes, downright cold-hearted. People will do things to you, hurt you, betray you, and tear away at the fabric of you as a human being. But, in all of that, we have a responsibility to forgive those who hurt us, abuse and mistreat us. Yeah, I know that forgiveness is not an easy thing for a lot of us, but for growth and healing, it's necessary.

Please allow me to explain why. Many times in life, people tend to do things without thinking, with the consequences of their actions being brutal. Most of these actions are perpetrated against the very people who they love and care for. Why is if oftentimes this way? ... That is the million dollar question. But they do it anyway, and in all truthfulness, we have a society of hurt people, existing from day to day, refusing to let go of that hurt that was done to them.

Many of those people have a hard time trusting others, never forgetting what was done to them. Many of those people feel that forgiving the offending party would be a great thing, but amazingly, they sometimes choose to hold onto the hurt and betrayal, because they feel that holding on to that negative energy empowers them, somehow. Never forgetting that hurt is a reminder of why they have hate in their hearts, and it will encourage them to never trust again. This is what people carry around with them on a daily basis. I'm here to say that is not a good thing. Living your lives like this is like putting arsenic or cyanide poisoning in your body, all the while, hoping that somehow, someone else will get sick. The only person that will be affected is you. Holding onto an unforgiving stance only affects the person holding to it, never the person who is guilty of dishing out the offense. That's just the way it has been and will continue to be.

Now, why do I say we have a responsibility to forgive? It's because we have a responsibility to ourselves to live the absolute best lives we can possibly live. When we refuse to forgive someone who has hurt us, we're not living our best lives. When you refuse to let go of a hurt, in essence, you're letting the person who hurt you live rent free in your mind. You constantly think about how they hurt you, why they hurt you, and sometimes you think of ways to get payback at that person or persons. When the negative energy of un-forgiveness lives in your being, it's almost like having an anchor shackled around your ankle and your life's progression is slow to move forward.

In some cases, you can develop illnesses in your body, due to refusing to forgive. If you've never heard this before, let me be the first to inform you; "your health is absolutely your first wealth". Think about what I'm saying here. You can possibly develop a health issue that no medicine on earth can probably heal you from, all because you are holding on to a past hurt or betrayal.

As I have said in the beginning of this chapter, letting go and forgiving someone who hurt you is not always easy, but here's the thing. When you forgive someone for hurting you, you're not doing it for that person's benefit;

you're doing it for your own benefit, always. Think of it this way. When you forgive, you release yourself from the negative energy that un-forgiveness can bring. You're not allowing that person to have power over your life, for they can and will have power over your life, even if they're dead and buried. Being willing to forgive every time you're wronged shows that you are a person of character and strength, and it shows that you refuse to give someone power over your life, no matter how bad they've hurt you. Remember, you have a responsibility to live the absolute best life you can possibly live. One of the most powerful ways to live your best life is by having the strength to forgive. This book is written with men in mind, but any and everyone can benefit from this.

Chapter Ten
Take Responsibility and Pride in Your Attire, Fellas

This chapter is especially meaningful and passionate to me in discussing a vital point in *Men=Responsibility*. I say it's important because this is where I discuss as best as I can, the importance of men taking pride in the clothes they wear and how they wear them. As a black man, I am starting to see on a regular basis, other men, mostly men of color, wear their pants in a sagging manner. Now while I do see men of other races occasionally wearing sagging pants, I see it mostly with young and somewhat older black men, quite often. This bugs me almost to the point that whenever I see it, my skin crawls with disgust. Without trying to be overly critical, I'll tell you why.

There was a time in life that when a man left his place of residence, he would have on a really nice suit, or a pressed shirt and some pressed slacks, looking professional and looking like he was ready to take care of some serious business. I'm talking back in the 1940's, 50's, and 60's. It was as if you could go to these men's closets and see what they would wear regularly and you were heavily impressed with their daily attire. One instance for me that comes to mind is the popular TV show "Perry Mason".

Whenever I watch this show, I always see the men wearing suits, ALL of them. No one was wearing anything sagging off of their bodies. They were smooth, they dressed sharp and they all looked responsible. Now, many of them were unsavory characters and you did not really find out how unsavory they were until the end of the episode, but that is a different subject. Fast forward from those days to these days... there has been a huge shift in that many men nowadays appear to lack pride in what they wear. You can be driving down the street and you'll see a group of men walking and almost all of them will have their pants sagging and/or their shirts wrinkled, not looking their best. Now, I'll attempt to explain the purpose behind this chapter.

Yes, this is a free country and people should be able to wear what they want: I am not arguing that point. The point I'm trying to make is that as men, we should want to look our best each and every time we leave our homes. A famous person who shall remain nameless once said in an interview, I believe that every man should dress nice for the sole purpose of impressing the ladies. He said that men should always take pride in wearing clothing that the ladies would like to see on them. He is right.

When a man is walking down the street, in a mall or in some other public area, with his pants sagging, this is not impressive to a real lady. If this look does impress some women, that should be a signal of a problem to the man. Moreover, on a personal note, no one wants to see a man's undergarments! I know I don't: furthermore, I don't want anyone seeing my undergarments, ever. And here's the big breakdown. They say that clothes don't make the man, and while that may be true to an extent, clothes do give people a certain perception of that man.

Here's an example of what I mean. You take two men, one smart and intelligent, and the other not so smart and not so charming and you stand them side by side. The smart man is wearing a dingy tank top and some sagging blue jeans with his underwear showing, and the man who's IQ is below smart, is wearing a Brooks Brothers suit and Ferragamo shoes. Even though you can't tell by looking at either man, who's smart and who's not smart, you can definitely see what they're wearing.

Now ask yourself honestly, who "looks" more presentable and responsible, the smart man wearing the tank top and sagging pants, or the dumb man wearing the suit and designer shoes? If you're smart and I know you are, you're going to say that the man wearing the suit looks the better of the two. Why, because perception matters in this society. More men need to understand this, when they are making decisions about whether or not to wear certain clothing.

People tend to gravitate to men who look like they are "casket sharp". He doesn't have to be an overly smart man, but when he's wearing clothes that display grace, pride and confidence, he'll be taken more serious than the person who is overly smart but dresses like he's in a gang. Don't misunderstand me, fellas. The goal in this chapter is not to be critical or judgmental. My goal is for men to see how important it is to be a better steward over what they wear. It's not easy to explain why society tends to judge a man based on his appearance, it is just the way it is.

Think about when a man goes on a job interview, and that man decides to go to that interview wearing clothes that do not put him in a light which is favorable to how he should be presenting himself as a professional. By all accounts, that man may be smart as Einstein, but when he shows up to be interviewed and the manager who's conducting the interview sees what he's wearing, that manager will no doubt think that he's not serious about getting this job. Why? Employers want to see everyone who desires to be hired present in a professional manner.

As that saying goes, "You only get one chance to make a great first impression". Presenting yourself in professional attire gives the impression that you're serious about being given the opportunity to get the job. Anything other than a professional look and your chances of being hired are slim to none. You can call that basic job skill 101. Professional attire gives any and everyone the impression that you mean business. This is the way of the world, my friend.

I'm going to share something my mother used to tell me all of the time, when I was younger. She would say to avoid being in a car with nothing but black men, riding four deep. I would ask her why she would tell me that. Her explanation was that it was not a good look. "Not a good look, ma?"

"No son…, not a good look for 4-5 young black men to be riding in the same car going somewhere". She went on to say that the perception of us, to a certain demographic of society is that we "look" like we're up to no good, especially to the police. How many times have cops pulled over a car full of black men, all because the cops believe that those young black men must be looking for trouble to get into? As crazy as this may sound, it's true, as I have experienced that very thing before in my life. While I won't get into the specifics of my personal experience, the point I want to make is that perception of what we as men wear and how we look does matter in this society.

While we can't control other people perceptions, we can control what we wear on our bodies. I believe that we have a responsibility to wear clothing that puts us at an advantage in life. It's doesn't matter if you're black or white, or any other nationality. If you're a man, then as a man you should want to dress in a way that makes you appealing to the public, even if you're not trying to be appealing. Because you never know what opportunity may present itself to you, just by looking suave and debonair.

Now, does this mean that after reading this chapter you should start dressing up everywhere you go? Well, that's entirely up to you as a man. My only purpose is to hopefully shed some light on how important perception is; to know that we as men are looked at and judged by many, based on the clothes we wear. It's not right nor is it cool, but that's just how it is in this life. Of course, you are going to continue to wear whatever you want to wear, but please understand that there are certain processes in life that we as men must embrace, and our attire is one important process.

Do yourselves a favor, men; take pride in your clothing. Believe it or not, your attire is extension of your character. You owe it to yourself to be taken seriously by others, so make it your responsibility that others are taking you seriously, even if they don't verbally express it.

Chapter Eleven
A Real Man Wants His Own Stuff

The title of this chapter speaks for itself. Any man, who is a real man, wants what belongs to him and not anyone else. He wants his own possessions in life, and that's how it should be, right? Well, this is not exactly how it always is, which is unfortunate. You see, one of the biggest reasons why I'm so passionate about seeing men embrace responsibility for their lives is because so many men seem passive and aloof about their lives; lacking the passion to live their best lives.

For example, you have men who would rather live in their parent's basement, rather than leave that basement and go out and get their own place. I'm talking about men in their 20's, 30's and even 40's. You have men who would rather depend on someone taking them places, or constantly borrowing someone else's vehicle, rather than doing what they can to acquire their own. Amazing, huh? There was a time in life when men took pride in being strong-minded, proud, and responsible men. They took pride in the sense of wanting their own everything: their own place to live, their own car or truck to drive, their own money to purchase whatever they desired to have; their own stuff. Somewhere along the way, many men have lost their way. That desire to have what they could call their own has disappeared.

Personally, I want to see men go back to that way of thinking. How can you call yourself a man and someone else is responsible for you making it in life? Now don't get me wrong, we sometimes need a helping hand to survive, but that helping hand should not be a constant thing in a man's life.

Speaking from experience, I had it tough in my life years ago. I was living in a rented room, barely struggling to survive. There were days where I didn't know where my next meal was coming from. But, despite my struggles, I managed to remember that I am a man, and that as a man, I had to do what I had to do in order to survive. Yes, I had help from different people and organizations, but I also realized that that help was temporary and that I had to step up my hustle. Many times I found myself working multiple jobs at the same time. It was tough at times, but, I soon realized that being a man meant doing things you don't want to do sometimes. In order for you to be accountable, that is what it takes.

I didn't want to call my mother or anyone else when things got tough. I had to figure out how I was going to get through that test, on my own, as a man. Not being prideful, but living the saying "a man's got to do what a man's got to do"... such a true statement. When a man reaches a certain age in life, he has to realize that he is in charge of his life and he is responsible for what happens in his life. Not his mother, father, grandparents, friends, or anyone else. The responsibility for his life falls on his shoulders. Fellas hear me and hear me good.

There is a sense of pride that comes when knowing that what you have in life is yours and no one else's. There is a feel good essence that comes when the place that you reside in and lay your head down at night is your place, and not your parents' or friend's home. Or the vehicle you drive, knowing that you pay the note on it because it's yours and you don't have to give it back to the owner. You're the owner of that vehicle, and that feels good to a man. And there is something else to consider as well. Even if people don't tell you this out right, there is an increased level of respect that others show you when you have your own. If people know that you're living your life based on what others are constantly doing for you, ~~and~~ you're a grown man, and you're not looked at as a real man, but as a loser and a good-for-nothing bum.

Fellas, don't expect a woman to take you serious, or for a woman to even want to look your way, if you don't have your own possessions in life. As I have stated in a previous chapter, women love a responsible man. A real man is going to be responsible enough to have his own place, his own car, his own money, his own everything. If you are a man that does not have what you need or want at the moment, make sure you're working to acquire it. Make sure that you're constantly taking some type of action to better your life. For crying out loud, fellas, avoid being lazy! Life is too short and too precious to be lazy. There are so many opportunities for betterment that surround us in life; too many for you not to be living your best life.

I'm imploring any man reading this book that may not be where he wants to be in life at present; whatever desires you have in life, work hard, dream big, sacrifice and do what it takes to have what you desire in life, so that you can be the man that people can and will respect. You owe it to yourself, fellas. So, get to it!! Be responsible and have your own stuff in life.

Chapter Twelve
She is NOT a Punching Bag, Fellas...She is a Lady

There was NO WAY that I could have written this book and not include a chapter on violence against women. I can say unequivocally that I am against a man hitting a woman. I'll never be down with that, for as long as I live. The only way an instance of such violence can be justified is if the man's life is in danger from the woman and he's acting in self-defense. According to some studies, less than 1% of domestic violence cases are reported to the police. The National Violence Against Women Survey for 2000 reported that 25% of women and 7.6% of men reported being victims of intimate partner violence at some point in their lives.

I guess for me, I can't imagine what would make a man puts his hands on a woman, in such a violent way. I understand that men and women have disagreements and arguments; they don't always see things the same way. But it's a terrible thing when an argument or disagreement turns violent and fists start flying, mainly his fists hitting her face or body. One of the best things a man can do when he finds himself in a situation with his wife/girlfriend where things are heated, is to walk away and cool off. Some women have a distinct way of pushing a man's buttons, and some men are so easily sent over the edge by a woman. But, I can tell you that hitting that woman out of anger is wrong, on so many levels.

Why is it wrong? Well, for starters, a man is stronger than a woman, and if he works out a lot, he can do some real damage to that woman. Secondly, and more importantly, fighting your woman tends to only make things worse, not better. I watched the movie "Straight out of Brooklyn" some years ago...part of the story had to do with domestic violence. The father in the movie was beating on the mother constantly, as if he felt that taking whatever aggression he had out on her was the way to go. Well, at one point in the movie, the mother's face was beating so badly, her employer had a complaint about it from a client who did not want someone who cleaned and cooked for them to look like they had went a few rounds with Mike Tyson.

You see, what the father of the movie was doing was not only horrible, but he was hindering his own household. If the mother could not work because she was beaten up so badly, and her employer suspended her due to her face looking bad, she could not bring home a paycheck, thus, limiting the household from having the extra much needed funds. His actions were hurting his family. He was definitely not displaying responsibility in this manner.
Any man who hits on his woman is not a responsible man, because a responsible man knows that hitting a woman is not what a real man does. Like the title of this chapter says, a woman is not a punching bag.

If a man has stored up aggression within himself, he should go to the gym and take that aggression out on an actual punching bag. Those things were created to absorb punishment from fists. No matter how hard you hit, punch, kick, or head butt a punching bag, you're not going to hurt it, because it's an inanimate object with no feelings whatsoever. That is not the case with a woman.

67

She is a human being with feelings and emotions. When you punch, kick, head butt or commit some act of violence against a woman, she feels that and will always feel it.

Men, if you're fortunate to have a lady in your life, you should see her as a gift, because that is what she is. I've been married for some years now, and not once have I ever thought about hitting my lovely wife; not once! Sure, we have our ups and downs, good times and bad ones, as well as our occasional rifts, but I could not look myself in the mirror if I was the type of man who would hit his wife. I'm stronger than she is. I have a mild fight background, meaning that if I were to ever get into a physical altercation with my wife, fighting would not be good for her. But thankfully, I'm responsible and I know better. I know that a real man would not ever want to hit a woman. This is what all men, young and old, need to realize and adhere to.

In addition to the physical violence that some men can carry out, it's also important that we as men watch the words we speak to our women as well. Only allow yourselves to speak uplifting words to the special lady in your life. This is extremely important, because words can cause long lasting damage, more than physical abuse can. A woman can heal from physical abuse somewhat faster than she can from verbal abuse. Be responsible for the things you say to your wives or girlfriends, fellas. They can carry what you say to them for a very long time, with the affects sometimes being very damaging.

Don't let your lady be a proverbial punching bag, via your fists or your mouth. Treat her right and she'll treat you right. Talk sweet to her and she'll give it back to you in spades. Trust me, fellas. Sadly, there will be continual, ongoing cases of domestic violence reported on. But, if this book can help a man understand why it's never okay to hit a woman or talk crazy to a woman, then this will be a wonderful plus, in so many ways.

I'll also add this in as well…. Fellas, if you find yourself in a relationship with a woman who likes to fight, squabble and keep conflict going on, then just know that this is not the type of woman you need to be with. Relationships should always be peaceful, joyous and happy, not full of ongoing conflict and grief. I have heard of some relationships where couples will argue and fight with each other, just so that they can have exciting make up sex afterwards. While that can be a unique way of being with someone, that way of operating can get old and tired real fast. Besides, who wants to argue and fight with the person they're with on an almost constant basis?

Any man who exhibits class, style, charisma and charm in his life should want a woman who exhibits those same traits as well. Having a woman in your life who likes to argue and fight is not someone who you can grow a healthy and vibrant relationship with. If, by chance, you and she should have a fight one day, she or your neighbor may call the police on you. If the cops see any physical bruises on her, guess who they're taking to jail?

Even if that woman started the fight, the police always look at the man as the stronger, more dominant figure; the one who can do more damage to her than she can to him. That's why it's important to get to know someone over a period of time, because you can't tell what type of person they REALLY are just by looking at them. Some of the most attractive women out here are some of the craziest and psychotic ones you'll ever come across; the ones who love fighting a man. Avoid those women, fellas, because they're only going to be burdensome in the long run, no matter how physically attractive they are.

Bottom line, a real man would never hit a woman, because women are not punching bags. Their bodies are not designed to take punishment from a man's fist. If you are the type of man who feels a woman needs to be smacked around from time to time, seek immediate counseling and get your mind right. Your life and your freedom may depend on this. Please believe me, ~~that~~ no woman is worth going to jail for or losing your life for. Be responsible men: ~~and~~ don't hit women!!

Chapter Thirteen
A Responsibility to Be Positive and Stay Positive

I get real pumped up and excited whenever I talk about thinking, living, speaking, and being positive. I just love encouraging and motivating people to live life to the fullest. With so much negative energy on the planet, we have a responsibility to embrace positivity; doing all that we can to stay in a positive space.

Now, let me talk about negativity for a moment. We live in a world where negative energy, negative vibes, negative spirits, and negative words constantly surround us. If you watch the news cycle on any given network regularly, you'll see that the stories are mostly negative. Isn't it amazing how the news channels normally report the seemingly 'happy' stories at the end of the news hour? The negative stories take up a lot of time, but the positive stories only get a few minutes of report time.

What about the people that we come into contact with on a daily basis? Most of them are always complaining about everything that's not right in their lives. It seems that the world is fueled by negativity, and it shouldn't be that way, but, nonetheless, this is the reality, more often than not. Understand this; it takes very little effort to be negative. You can stand in the middle of Times Square, New York City for example, you can feel negativity from the millions of people that will walk past you and by the end of the day, you will have absorbed almost all of that negative energy you were surrounded by.

Here is another thing you have to be careful about as well, when it comes to people, even family and friends: You can find yourself having a conversation with someone, while your day can be going great and wonderful, but the person you're talking to is having a bad day, with negative things going on in their lives. If you make the mistake of allowing that person to dump onto you all that is happening in their lives, from a negative standpoint, all of their negative talk and complaining, that energy will ultimately transfer to you.

As a result, you will no doubt find yourself feeling bad and dreary. In other words, the negativity that the other person is holding on to, will eventually seep into your consciousness, if you allow it. You have to guard yourself from that type of energy, because none of it is good energy. Every day should be a day in which we allow positive things to happen to us. A wonderful way to do that is by avoiding negativity, at all costs.

Now, I'm not at all saying you shouldn't want to listen to a person's drama and/or woes, especially if they need someone to talk to. But, what I am saying is if you are always receiving negative energy without dispensing positive energy in return, you will find that you're starting to view life through the negative prism that others view it from. This is something you can't allow to happen.

Now, let's talk about positivity and why I say it's a responsibility to stay positive. By steadily allowing yourself to stay around positive people and positive surroundings, what you're doing is allowing your spirit to stay healthy and powerful. We already are inundated with negative things. Therefore, why should you allow that stuff to permeate your essence? You simply should not. When you do, your days will start off on the wrong foot, lacking the admonition that every day you are blessed to see is a precious gift. The last thing you should want in your life is negativity. So, here is what you need to do for a positive atmosphere to be yours always.

First, only think positive thoughts. Allow what you hear and see to be positive things, words and images. Go to your library or favorite book store and search out authors who specialize in promoting positive living. Read books where positivity is at the forefront of what you read.

Next, only allow yourselves to hear and speak positive words. One important thing to understand about words is that they're powerful things. Negative words will tear down and destroy things, while positive words will build up and purify whatever direction they're aimed at. So, when you find yourself in some place where negative words are being spoken, get away from that area as quickly as you can. You don't want any of that negative talk / action to affect your day in the least bit.

You want each day you see to be a wonderful and vibrant day and you want to hear things that will enable you to have a wonderful and positive day. Speak positive words over your life and your days. Say out loud to yourself, "This is my day and I will be successful in this day". Think about it. If more people did this before their days started, they would feel great and all negativity would leave their presence immediately.

Also, it's important to have a circle of friends who embrace being positive on a daily basis. You're familiar with the old adage, "Birds of a feather flock together"? This is true in every sense, and you'll see people who tend to think alike hanging out together. You can't find yourself being positive, hanging out with a bunch of negative people. That is a bad mixture that will never work. Remember, this book has everything to do with being responsible, so you have a responsibility to yourself to always stay positive and to surround yourself with positive people and atmospheres.

Always think positive, always speak positive, and always hear positive words and phrases. Read positive books and fill your heart and spirit with nothing but positive things, constantly. If you do these things, you are investing in your future and no matter what anyone says, you're bound to have a long, fruitful and adventurous life, filled with nothing but positivity… the way life is supposed to be lived. You can do it, but it's your responsibility to make it happen. So, what are you waiting for? Make being and staying positive a priority in your life, now!!

Chapter Fourteen
Sacrifice: A man's got to Do What a Man's Got to Do

This chapter is particularly for all men who love to dream for bigger and better pursuits for their lives. I want to tell all of you men that there is absolutely NOTHING wrong with dreaming. We all have dreams, big ones and bigger ones. I am always encouraging people to follow their dreams, chase their dreams, solidify their dreams, and live their dreams. But, while you're going after those dreams, you have to remember the "right now". What do I mean by the "right now" you may ask? Well, it's simple. The "right now" is the present time. It's being cognoscente of the important things of the moment.

I'll explain what I mean in this manner: When I was a young teenager, I would always say out loud the things that I wanted to accomplish when I got older. I would tell my mama about my dreams and desires. She, of course, would be happy about my ambitions. However, she would always say to me, "Son, I hear you loud and clear, but what about the meantime, in between time". Sometimes she would make me angry when she would say that because I felt she was disregarding what I was saying. But, then she would explain what she meant. She would tell me that while it was important to have big dreams and aspirations, I had to remember the things I had to take care of in the present, like paying bills and making money to buy food. You know the things that responsible people take care of because that is what responsible people do. If I was going to eat, have a phone, have a car and eventually have my own place to live, I had to be prepared to take care of those things, in the present time. This is what I want to explain in this chapter, for the men who are the non-stop dreamers in the world.

A great example that I can come up with is the TV show "Divorce Court". In my opinion, this show premiers some of the most off-the-wall characters you will ever see in everyday living. Even though it's not a real divorce court, it's interesting to watch and for the most part, very entertaining. Most of the people that appear as litigants on the show are so crazy. It's funny, and it touches on everything that most couples deal with. From infidelity to not working a regular job, to finding out if the paternity of a baby is on the level. It's all there for the world to see.

Now, the main thing that really gets me riled up are some of the men that appear on the show, and the belief they have that when they get married, their wives are the only ones who have to be responsible in the marriage. That's right; I have heard many guys say things that put the oneness solely on the woman. Things like "She's responsible for the kids", or "She makes sure that the bills are paid on time". Silly things of that nature and what are the men doing, while the women are the ones being responsible?

The men are following their dreams and desires to become rappers, club promoters, business owners, or whatever their hearts desire. They are following their dreams while the wives assume the responsibility of the household, and I'm here to tell you that this is wrong!!! Why is it wrong? It is wrong because while there is nothing wrong with the men pursuing their dreams, the men should be taking the lead to make certain that things are well and prosperous in the household.

This is what I mean when I say *Men=Responsibility*. It is the responsibility of the man, the husband, the leader of the household, to be responsible for the bills being paid, for putting food on the table, putting gas in the cars, and whatever else men should do as men. Fellas, hear me good. I know some of you don't liking working 9-5 jobs that don't fit your personality, but as a man, you have to work and provide for your families. That means you work and sacrifice and do what is necessary for the prosperity of you and yours. If you have to work a job sweeping floors, or selling cars, or waiting tables, you do what you have to do to be responsible and to take care of the ones you love.

You can't call yourself a man and put the responsibility of maintaining a household squarely on the shoulders of the woman. That is not what a REAL man is going to do. The woman is the helpmate. That means she helps out and takes up the slack when it's needed. In other words, she backs up her man. But, first and foremost her man is taking the lead and taking care of his responsibilities as a man. I am going to give a shout out to a chef friend of mine. I've known this man for some years now, and he is what I would call the consummate family man. I haven't had a chance to tell him yet, but I have so much respect and admiration for how he carries himself as a family man.

He's on Facebook quite often, and every time I see his posts, he's working and earning $$ or spending time with his wife and kids!! That's right; he's working some kitchen job, whether it's out of town or here in the city, locally. If I know this brother like I think I do, he's taking that money he makes home to his wife and kids. No matter what ever needs to happen for his family, he's going to make sure that he as the head of his household he takes care of that matter.

Obviously, he knows that the well-being of his family is his sole responsibility. Overall, I respect how this man is always willing to sacrifice for his family at the drop of a dime, no matter what it takes, and you can't help but to respect that in a man. I don't want to mention your name bro, but just know that I salute you man. Don't you ever stop being a shining example of real manhood and responsibility.

I said all of this to say that as a man, if you have a family, that family is your responsibility, bottom line. It is an extra added bonus to have a wife / helpmate who is capable, willing and able to do whatever she can to aid and assist in the betterment of the daily functions of the home, as a whole. But, the first line of defense should always rest with the man of the house. The man of the house should always make certain that things are taken care of. A real man will take pride in that. It should make a man feel less than a man when his woman is the main one responsible for the family being taken care of.

My encouragement to the men on this one is this: take serious inventory of your life and priorities right away, and if you're not being responsible in regards to making sure that your household is your responsibility, change that and change it now. If you don't change that, you may end up finding yourself by yourself. Never stop following your dreams, but take care of the things that matter now! Sacrifice will always be at the core of manhood, and a man has to be willing to sacrifice. There is no other way around that truth. A man's got to do what a man's got to do. A man has got to be responsible, bottom line.

Chapter Fifteen
Don't Cheat on Her. Just Be a Man and Tell Her the Freaking Truth!!

Now, this chapter is where I'm probably going to piss some of the fellas reading this book off..., but as a man, I believe that I have a mandate to tell other men this, so here goes. A responsible man is going to conduct himself in a respectable manner at all times. In doing so, he is not going to cheat on his wife or girlfriend. Yeah, I said it!!! The responsible man is a man who is not a philanderer or a cheater. The responsible man is someone who is faithful to the ONE woman he is with currently. If that man should find that things are not going well in his relationship with that one woman, then he will exhibit responsibility and either try to work things out with her, or he will break up with her and then move on to another woman.

I know it sounds like I'm lecturing here, but in all honesty, men need to hear this. One of the reasons I believe men cheat is because they know they can and most women these days would rather have half of a man than a whole man. What I mean when I say "half of a man" is that specific man more than likely belongs to another woman, a wife or girlfriend. This is not meant to roll the bus over the women, but the truth is the truth. Some women would rather share a man with another woman than to have her own man. (Or, she may settle in the notion that she can't have a man who is all and only hers alone.) In certain cities in the US, the ratios of women to men is astounding, with some being 4 women to 1 man. Most men know this, and so they figure that they can't possibly maintain with just one woman, right?

Well, I'm here to tell you that men who think like that are in the wrong from jump. It's simply not responsible for any man to jungle more than one woman, but most do so and have been doing so for centuries. For most men, having multiple women is empowering and it makes him feel big, but like I said, it's not responsible. Let's get into why it's not responsible. Most women, when they're in a relationship or marriage, they want to feel like they're the only one that man is with. They want to feel like he's being faithful and honest with them. They want to believe he's not two-timing them in the least bit. More than all of this, women want to believe that he, the man they're with, is being responsible and accountable to them and them only.

One important reason why men who behave in an unbecoming manner are not responsible has to do with honesty. No one likes to deal with a dishonest person, because you can't believe a word they say. Any man who cheats on his lady, whatever her title is, is a dishonest man, straight up. What makes him dishonest you ask? Well for one, if he's out with his "side piece" when his main lady calls him on his phone and asks him where he is, and he tells her he's out with ~~is~~ his boys or working late, he's being dishonest. He clearly doesn't want his main lady knowing he's with another woman.

Now, there may be a myriad of reasons as to why he's cheating on his main lady with another woman, but any way you look at it, he's not being responsible. If he were responsible, he would ~~either~~ not be cheating in the first place and/or he would be with his main lady, having fun and doing things couples do. Being dishonest, lying about your whereabouts, and not being truthful is an integral part of what hurts a man's standing in being responsible in his life. And here is another thing that I find so puzzling about most men. They would rather live a lie than to be truthful. In that I mean live a lie and have a wife or girlfriend, and have other women on the side, rather than to tell their wives or girlfriends the truth. Being a man means us as men have to be responsible, and in being responsible, we have to tell the truth in our lives.

Don't misunderstand me men, women do cheat as well, but let's be real about this. If so many men didn't cheat and deceive and two-time, most women might not be inclined to do so. That is one of the main reasons why it seems like I'm so hard on men. We men are the catalysts for many things that happen in life…. Our actions can be the cause of some of the reactions that we may not want to see happen.

Remember the TV show "Cheaters"? I remember when that show first aired. It has shown countless numbers of people caught with someone other than the person they were either in a relationship with or married to. The major thing that stood out is when the guilty person was caught on camera and exposed for the world to see, they didn't have a viable explanation as to why they were with another person. That's just it men!! There really is no viable or acceptable reason ever to suffice for cheating on someone. The reality is that when a man cheats, he's being selfish: ~~and~~ he is only thinking about his own selfish desires. He never really thinks about the damage he's causing. On a personal note, I detest cheating, in any form.

I believe it's possible for a man to be faithful to one woman, but, he has to *choose* to be faithful. It all comes down to choice. When you cheat, you choose not to be responsible, and when you don't cheat and can be truthful in your life, you're choosing responsibility. Now, some may argue with me and say that a man can be responsible and cheat on his lady. I say that is bull crap! He's not being responsible because he's not being real with himself. The cheating man has to act a certain way around all of the women he's frolicking with. He's wearing a different mask with each woman he entertains, and that mask is concealing the real person he truly is.

Listen, all I can do is encourage men to do better in being responsible in their lives. It's not lost on me that men will never really give up cheating, but I can't see how it can hurt for a dude like me to tell men to not cheat and just be honest with the women in their lives. If you're not happy in your relationship fellas, don't cheat. If the woman you're with is not making you happy anymore, talk to her and let her know how you're feeling, but don't cheat. If your lady is gaining some weight and she's not looking like she used to look when you first met her, take her to the gym and you both work out like a happy couple, just don't cheat. If you see that the relationship is not fun like it used to be, work hard to put that spark back into the relationship. Be spontaneous, and don't cheat. Tell the woman that you're with the truth about whatever is going on with you and her: don't be afraid to tell the truth.

If things are not reparable between the two of you, as a couple, I'm certain that the woman would rather you break things off with her completely than to pretend things are well, all the while you're cheating on her, spending time with other women, all while lying to her repeatedly about where you are or who you're with. The interesting thing about cheating is at some point, men tend to mess up and the women find out anyway, resulting in the man's whole cover being blown off and exposed.

My whole point in this chapter is to engage men who are either cheating right now or have cheated in the past as to why not just be honest with her and just let her know you are not happy, instead of playing games and being dishonest.

Also, for the men who are not having any problems in their marriages or relationships, but still feel the urge to be with other women as well, just know that no woman wants to share you with another woman. Think of it like this, fellas. What if your woman had another man that was "servicing" her on the side as well? What if your woman was the type that flirted with other men, and exchanged phone numbers with other men? What if your woman liked to engage in "revenge cheating" because she got tired of you stepping out on her, cheating with other women? All of that would drive you nuts, and it would drive you nuts because most men can't stand the thought of another man touching his wife or girlfriend. So men, if you know you don't want another man in your woman's life, what makes you think she wants another woman in her life? The bottom line is this: if you want her to be loyal, faithful, truthful and honest with you, then you should be responsible and give her the same consideration and respect, on all fronts. It's not worth it to cheat on your women, men, it never is. Be a real man, be truthful, be honest, be respectable, be accountable and be responsible.

Chapter Sixteen
Why It Is Important to Always Be Responsible

Between the ages of 1 to 18, someone is responsible for that baby/boy/teenager. But when that man-child hits an age where he no longer needs someone to be responsible for him; this is when he enters the time where he's inundated with responsibilities. Now, the question is; 'why is it always important for a man to be responsible'? Well, if a man is not being accountable in his life, why does he exist? Why is he here, alive and walking around?

You see, a grown man has so many responsibilities in his life, especially if that man desires to have a family, possessions and to be relevant in life. Like I said, when he's a small boy, someone is responsible for him. But, when he's no longer a boy, but now a man, he is now the one responsible for his life, or he should be. If a man is not responsible, everything in his life will be in shambles, out of whack, and unbalanced.

Now, what are some things that show a lack of responsibility in a man? A man who doesn't pay his bills on time, is one of them. I'll give an example. Say you're in your home, enjoying a wonderful evening with your family. It's a hot summer day, and you have the air conditioning running; everyone is relaxing. All of a sudden the power shuts off... there's confusion as to why there is no power. The fridge is off; there are no lights, no power whatsoever. Then, the wife asks the husband "Babe, did you remember to pay the light bill?" All of a sudden it hits him. "Dang, I forgot to pay the bill". Well, we all know what happens when you don't pay the light bill. The power company shuts that power off, and for however long until the bill is paid, the power remains off. Now, here's the kicker. Whenever you do pay the bill after the power has been temporarily shut off, you have to wait until the company turns the power back on, and that can take hours. I'm speaking from experience here.

This guy forgot to pay the bill four days ago, so while enjoying an evening at home with family, the power gets shut off. You see, we as men have to not only be on top of things like this, but we also have to remember to be responsible for things like this. Fellas, our families depend on us to be responsible and we can't let them down or we end up suffering, even if the suffering is short lived. Paying bills is just one of the many aspects of being responsible as a man.

Even on your jobs, your employer expects you to be responsible. If you as a man are working at some place where you have been given tasks to complete on a daily basis, your supervisor/boss fully expects you to complete those tasks; not for you to have your co-worker or someone else do them for you. You are the responsible person that was hired to do your job, and if you show them that you can't be trusted to be responsible, then you can't expect to work there very long.

Take this into consideration as well. When you develop a reputation for being a certain way, as positions of employment are concerned, that reputation can follow you, whether it's a good reputation or a bad one. For instance, if you were unreliable, undependable, and not responsible on the last job you had, and you apply for new employment somewhere else, you may find yourself in a position where this new place may not want to hire you. Why? Because they got in contact with your last employer and that employer did not give a glowing endorsement of you and your character.

Upon hearing your former employer say that you were neither responsible nor reliable, what are the chances that the potential new employer will hire you? Straight up zero chances. That's rough, but that's how it goes in life as a grown up. Being responsible matters so much that being the opposite can hinder your progression. Believe me, no one wants to deal with a person who is not responsible. Now, on the flip side of that, is someone who is responsible: someone who can be depended on to carry out his work, and someone who is trustworthy and reliable. Men like this will always go far in life; he will receive promotions, bonuses, chances to advance and many other wonderful perks. The responsible man will be someone that everyone will look to, to get things done, because they know that he's responsible.

Being a man means you must be responsible. Life for you is easier, less stressful and more enjoyable when you're responsible. Of course, trials and tests come to us all, even when we're doing what we need to do to be responsible. But when we are purposely being responsible, those trials and tests can't break us: they won't last long. Again, the question was 'why is it important to always be responsible'?

Because, if you're a real man and you want to be taken seriously, as a man, then you'll be the type of man that when it comes to living your best life and enjoying things that men tend to enjoy (family, money, personal possessions, etc.), you understand that there is a responsibility in maintaining those things and you'll always be up for the challenge. Men, bottom line, your life moves forward in a positive fashion when you make it a priority to be responsible. This is what being a man is all about.

Chapter Seventeen
No Excuses!!

Have you ever heard the saying "people who make excuses don't make progress, and people who make progress don't make excuses"? Well, if you haven't heard this statement, just know that it is a true statement. Men who are responsible in life don't have time for excuses, because they know that excuses are useless, absolutely useless. Men who are responsible in life have time for one thing: progression. Men who are responsible have time for moving forward, getting things accomplished, having successful lives and families. That's what real men have time for; nothing else. Now, for the following questions I'm posing here below, ask yourself these questions; see if you fit the mold of being responsible on a daily basis.

1. Am I someone that my family can depend on to handle what a man is supposed to handle, whatever that is?
2. Am I the type of man who takes initiative in life, or do I need to be pushed to do things?
3. Do I like where I am in life… if not, what responsible moves am I making to propel my life to a happier place?
4. Can ten people who know me well tell others that I'm a responsible man?
5. Am I a responsible man where my money is concerned… if not, how can I do better in not being irresponsible in that regard?
6. Am I responsible to always dress for success: do I always take pride in my appearance, no matter where I go in my daily life?

7. Am I a responsible husband to my wife, as well as a responsible father to my children?
8. Am I the type of person who is prone to forgive or do I tend to hold grudges?
9. Am I responsible when it comes to my sex life? Do I value my life and the lives of others, with regard to STD's, etc?
10. Am I responsible to pay for my own way in life, or do I depend on others to pay for whatever I need or want?
11. Do I even care in the least about being responsible or do I enjoy living life on the edge without a care about my present or future?
12. Will I begin to impart traits of responsibility into our youth, so that they can have a good foothold in life? Do I even care about the youth?

These are questions you can ask yourselves on a daily basis, to give yourselves a 'self-awareness check', on behalf of all of the wonderful women out here that have sons, brothers, nephews, male friends and so forth. Please, share this book with any one whom you feel could use a wonderful piece of information on the importance of being responsible and always taking responsibility for their actions.

There is so much involved in being a "man", but one of the most important aspects of being a man is to be a RESPONSIBLE man. Why? Because you're depended on to be responsible, from the ladies you court and eventually marry, to the children you have and are to raise as respectable and responsible adults, extended to your jobs and businesses. So much is riding on your being a responsible man. So go forth men and get to work on being more responsible. That is your obligation as a man. In addition, take this with you: if you're not a responsible man, you're not a REAL MAN.

Remember, you stall your growth and progression with excuses, but you completely eliminate excuses, as you work toward real growth and progression. The choice is yours, so choose wisely, because so much is at stake. There is NO EXCUSE for a man not to embrace being responsible in his life. Make a decision to be responsible and go do it!! Be well, fellas; always embracing your true manhood, by being responsible.

Bonus Chapter
Never Mind What "They" Think About You or Say About You

I've decided to add this chapter solely as an encouragement piece to those dealing with the stigma of living their lives based on other people's opinion of them. Here's the thing with that. No matter how hard you try, no matter how much work you put into it, you are not going to be able to please everyone. It just can't be done. I'm not the kind of guy that goes around and says what can't be done, but this is just one of those things that simply can't be done.

Someone will always complain about you, gripe about you, find fault with you and be critical of you in some way. You can be someone who does most things close to perfect, but it almost never fails that someone, somewhere will be critical of you. As humans, we tend to let what others say about us affect us, infusing unnecessary weight in our lives. I'm here to encourage you to not live your life that way.

Here is my reason for saying this: before I get into the whys, let's talk about who "they" are. They are your family members, your so-called friends, your co-workers, your social media buddies. They can be anyone close to you or somewhat close to you. Most of us have those people that we confide in and tell our deepest feelings and secrets to. Most of us have a deep love for "they", and we care about what "they" say to us..., we care about their opinions of us, and how "they" feel about us.

Now, here is where I delve further into how "they" can be poisonous to us, for the most part. Those "they" that I described don't always support us or have our best interest at heart. Oftentimes, "they" don't always believe in us or our dreams, because "they" couldn't do something or get something accomplished in their own lives. Now, when "they" find out that you want to do something that "they" tried to do and failed, "they" will "hate" on you and try to discourage you from getting that thing done, no matter what it is. "They" will say things and use words to try and sway you from your goals.

Please understand that not all people close to you will do this, but there are those that will. What I'm saying here is with regard to those people that will discourage you, avoid them. Avoid them like the plague, as best as you can. Now, here's why you should not ever let what "they" say or think about you affect you. Life is short and it is a precious thing. You cannot afford to let ANYONE, regardless as to whom they are, steal or take away from you the pleasure of enjoying life to the fullest and taking advantage of all life has to offer.

None of us are perfect. We're always going to mess up in this life. The most important thing to realize is that you can only live your life for one person, YOURSELF. People are going to talk about you, no matter what. Thus, you can't do anything about those doing the talking, so I say go ahead and live life on the grandest platform that you can find. Whatever dreams you have, chase them down, tackle them, make them a reality and live them out! Don't ever allow the opinions of others to deter you from living your best life. Never mind what "they" think or say about you.

You should develop the mindset that it's none of your business what others say or think about you, because you're too busy living your best life to waste time on them, the "they". You have a responsibility to yourself, and that responsibility should be to enjoy your life.

Think of it like this; if their opinions won't pay your rent, car note, day care payments, mortgage or other bills, then those opinions shouldn't matter, right? Absolutely right, so pay them no mind, man. And like the saying goes, "Opinions are like anuses, everybody has one". Focus on your dreams and all that you desire to have in life. Do what you can to pay no attention to 'naysayers' and the doubtful bunch. You are responsible to your life, not the "they".

I will close this by saying that you only have one life to live, so live it up to the fullest; only allowing those who will edify and build you up to be in your circle. If people can't do that for you, then you don't need them anywhere around you, because they may very well be "dream killers". Avoid those "dream killers", and success can be yours for the taking. You and you alone are responsible for making all of your dreams come true. You can do it, now go and get it done!!!!

Extra Bonus Chapter
Positive Affirmations to Develop and Maintain a "Responsibility" Mindset

This extra chapter is what I call "Man Mantras". What I want to do with this one is to help you as a man grow and develop a mindset for wanting to be responsible in your life. The definition of <u>affirmation</u> is the act of affirming or asserting or stating something. When you make an affirmation, what you are doing is affirming something to be true or steadfast in your life. The affirmation can be positive or negative, and of course I will present a list of positive affirmations that you can say out loud to yourself on a daily basis.

Now, why is this important you may ask? Well, there is power in the words that come out of our mouths. When we say something, the words we speak tend to take shape in our lives. Words can build up, or tear down. Words can motivate our minds, shape our minds and cause our lives to go in the direction of that in which we speak. Most of the times, people unknowingly say things out of their mouths on a daily basis that put their lives in a bad place. Many times people don't even realize that what they've been saying is the cause of their lives being so tough and challenging.

When it comes to this business of being responsible, I am going to list some wonderful affirmations that you can say that I believe will help you grow as a man. No matter what anyone tells you, affirmations do indeed work. These affirmations can help you a great deal in developing a mindset of being more responsible in your lives, in the lives of your families, and other areas that we as men tend to need help in. Remember, you are the captain of the ship of your life, and your tongue is like the rudder of that ship.

The words you speak out of your mouth will always determine the direction of that ship, in a good and positive way or in a bad and negative way. Say these affirmations out loud to yourself and watch your mindset change, but you have to believe that it will. In addition, say these affirmations with excitement and fervor, like you mean it, because you do mean it.

1. I am a responsible man!
2. I am always responsible to handle what needs to be handled!
3. I always embrace my responsibilities, and I don't run from my responsibilities, no matter what!
4. I am responsible to always dress with class and dignity!
5. People can depend on me to be responsible at all times!
6. I am responsible to maintain my own household and to provide for my family, all of the time!
7. I am a responsible father to all of my children, always!
8. I am responsible with my money: I don't waste money frivolously!
9. I am responsible to pay my bills on time!
10. Responsible men don't hit women. Therefore, I don't hit women, ever!
11. I am responsible to work and provide for myself. That is my responsibility, no one else!

12. Being responsible equals being successful. Therefore, I am responsible and I am successful!
13. Nothing or no one will ever keep me from being responsible!
14. Every day I choose to be responsible!
15. I am responsible to not be a philanderer or a cheater!
16. I have a responsibility to be fair and honest with people, and to do right by people, as I embrace that responsibility for my life every day!
17. Being responsible makes me a winner in life; therefore, I am responsible every day of my life!

Now, whichever one of these positive affirmations apply to your life currently, speak them out of your mouth as often as you can. These powerful words will empower your mind and help you maintain a mindset of responsibility; propelling your life in a direction that you can and will be proud of. I assure you, these affirmations can help you, but the choice is up to you to let allow them to do so. This book is my contribution to society to help men become more responsible in their lives. Enjoy this book, fellas, and I'll see all of you at the top!!!

CPSIA information can be obtained
at www.ICGtesting.com
Printed in the USA
FFOW01n0055291117
43835153-42781FF

9 780692 973585